The How-To Handbook

The How-To Handbook

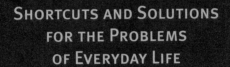

SHORTCUTS AND SOLUTIONS
FOR THE PROBLEMS
OF EVERYDAY LIFE

MARTIN OLIVER AND
ALEXANDRA JOHNSON

ZEST
BOOKS.

First published in 2013 by Zest Books
35 Stillman Street, Suite 121, San Francisco, CA 94107
www.zestbooks.net
Created and produced by Zest Books, San Francisco, CA

© 2013 Martin Oliver and Alexandra Johnson
Illustrations on pages 33, 58, 59, 68, 69, and 70 © Zoe Zuniga.
Illustrations on pages 16, 19, 21, 25, 26, 27, 30, 31, 36, 37, 38, 40, 41, 42, 43, 44, 45,
46, 49, 50, 51, 57, 63, 68, 71, 72, 74, 75, 78, 79, 83, 88, 89, 90, 91, 97, 98, 99, 100, 101,
102, 106, 107, 108, 109, 110, 111, 117, 121, 122, 123 © Buster Books.
Illustrations on pages 13, 16, 18, 19, 52, 53, 55, 60, 61, 62, 64, 65, 67, 73, 86, 87, 93,
94, 95, 96, 103, 104, 113, 114, 115, 116, 120 © Karen Donnelly.

Young Adult Nonfiction / Health & Daily Living/Daily Activities
Library of Congress control number: 2012943316
ISBN: 978-1-936976-34-8

Interior and cover design: Tanya Napier

Manufactured in the U.S.A.
DOC 10 9 8 7 6 5 4 3 2 1
4500405465

Every effort has been made to ensure that the information presented is accurate.
The publisher disclaims any liability for injuries, losses, untoward results, or any
other damages that may result from the use of the information in this book.

Connect with Zest!
zestbooks.net/blog
zestbooks.net/contests
twitter.com/ZestBooks
facebook.com/ZestBook
facebook.com/BookswithaTwist
pinterest.com/ZestBooks

Contents

PART 3: Get to Know Your Kitchen

PART 4: Clean Up Like a Pro

PART 5: Do It Yourself

PART 6: Emergency Skills 101

Introduction

How to Become Master of the Universe (or at least Master of your Own Well-Being)!

We aren't born knowing how to tie our shoes, drive a car, or even put on our own pants (after all, should we do it one leg at a time, or two?). These are all basic, essential skills that we need to learn in order to become fully operational—but this knowledge doesn't just fall from the sky. *The How-To Handbook* is a comprehensive guide to managing everyday challenges and doing all of these things efficiently, thoroughly, and *well*. Some of these skills may seem deceptively simple (like loading a dishwasher properly), while others may seem nearly impossible at the outset (like folding a fitted sheet—because how on earth are you supposed to fold something that has rounded corners and is designed to crumple up?!). So in the end, whether you're wondering about making it through the morning without burning your toast or escaping disaster in the great outdoors, we've got you covered.

The six sections of the book are organized to help you to quickly find the type of skill you want to master—from ironing a pair of pants in the "Looking (and Smelling)

Good" section to fixing a punctured tire in the "Do It Your-self" section, to cleaning your room quickly and well in the "Clean Up Like a Pro" section. Each skill is also broken down into a few simple steps and most are supplemented with images to help illustrate the finer points of the job.

But be warned: The smoother you handle life's little moments of chaos, and the more adept you become at managing all of life's *little* obstacles, the more likely people are to turn to you for help. That can be a burden sometimes, sure, but as James Bond continues to demonstrate in sequel after sequel, there are few things cooler than an assured bearing, a steady hand, and the confidence of knowing how to get things done.

WARNING

The information in these boxes will help alert you to some under-appreciated dangers and enable you to stay safe, no matter what.

As you make your way through this handbook, you'll come across these bonus tips that will help you master the various skills.

Part 1
Everyday Essentials

Do you get a little *too* freaked out when you see a spider? Do you have trouble packing for even an overnight trip? Are you always cramming for tests at the last minute? Panic no more! This first section won't just teach you how to wrap a gift or speak in public, it will teach you how to do these things really *well*. And armed with these basic skills, you'll be able to take a little bit more control of your life—and help out friends and family when they run into some of these roadblocks themselves (because there's still a sizeable chunk of humanity that doesn't know how to wrap a gift—let alone manage money!).

ADDRESS AN AUDIENCE

It can be totally nerve-wracking to speak in front of a large group of people (or even a small group sometimes)—and imagining the audience in their underwear is a little weird, right? Don't let stage fright get the best of you though. Follow these tips to feel more comfortable the next time you have to give a presentation.

● ●

1 Prepare your speech in advance. Even if you only have a few minutes' warning, try to go somewhere quiet to get your thoughts in order.

2 If memorizing your speech isn't an option, make short notes on index cards to remind you of the key points. Try not to rely on these notes too much though—looking down at the paper all the time can make you look nervous.

3 Rehearse your speech on your own before you say it in front of an audience. Pay special attention to any unfamiliar names you might have to say, or complicated thoughts you have in mind—the more you practice, the less likely you are to get tongue-tied or lost.

4 When you give your speech, try not to walk around or fidget. Take your time and talk slowly and clearly. If you make a mistake, stop and give yourself time to recover.

5 Smile and look toward your audience. Don't be afraid to make eye contact with individuals in the crowd—it can really help your speech make more of an impact.

AVOID MOTION SICKNESS

Nothing ruins a ride like nausea. But wait, and put down that entire bottle of Pepto! And the next time you're on a plane, boat ride, road trip, or runaway horse, bear these tips in mind instead.

● ●

Do: Drink plenty of water throughout the ride to help you stay hydrated.

Don't: Read, text, or play computer games. Looking down will make you feel sicker.

Do: Get plenty of fresh air if you can. Open a window in the car or walk up on deck on a boat. Unfortunately, opening a window isn't exactly an option on a plane.

Don't: Eat greasy or sweet snacks before you travel.

Do: Eat or drink ginger- or peppermint-flavored foods or drinks.

Don't: Look out at other moving cars if you're traveling in a car. Instead, try to focus on a fixed point on the horizon.

Seating Solution

In a car: Call shotgun! Sit in the front passenger seat if you can. Hey, then you can also be in charge of the radio!

On a boat: Sit up on the top deck, so you're in the fresh air.

On a plane: Get a seat over a wing, if possible, where it's the least bumpy.

BANISH HICCUPS

Hiccups can be embarrassing, frustrating, and definitely annoying. But the next time you get the hiccups, try one of these tricks to make them go away.

● ●

☆ Take a deep breath and hold it for as long as you can (but don't pass out!). Repeat until the hiccups stop.

☆ Swallow as quickly and as often as you can, or gulp little sips of water quickly.

☆ Eat a large spoonful of peanut butter.

☆ Swallow a spoonful of sugar.

☆ Suck on something sour, like a lemon or lime slice.

☆ Simultaneously plug your ears and swallow some water slowly.

BE SAFE IN A CITY

If you're not used to walking around in the city, you might stick out like a sore thumb (say "hello!" to pickpockets and "good-bye!" to your iPhone!). Read on to learn how to protect your things and yourself!) when visiting a city.

● ●

DUDE, WHERE'S MY MONEY??

Do: Keep your wallet close to you—either in the front pocket of your pants or in your bag. Make sure your bag is zipped up or buttoned. If you have a messenger bag or purse with a flap, keep the flap facing you to make it more difficult for someone to reach a hand in.

Don't: Pull out a wad of cash or credit cards in a crowded area, even if it's just a bunch of singles or your grocery store savings card. People will see that you have cash and cards, and you don't want to offer any additional incentive to potential thieves.

Do: Limit what you carry with you. Having your wallet, cell phone, iPod, Kindle, and other gadgets on your person leaves you wide open to theft. If you don't think you'll need it, don't bring it with you.

Don't: Take all your stuff out in plain sight. If you need to repack your bag, try to wait until you're in a quiet or relatively safe area. And never put your bag down unattended; always keep it with you or on you at all times if you want to keep it!

⚠ **WARNING**

NEVER get into a car with strangers, even if they say they'll take you home, and even if they don't seem sketchy at first glance. "Stranger danger" may sound silly but it's a real thing.

HOW DID THE HUMAN CROSS THE ROAD?

Do: Always cross the street in the crosswalk at an intersection, even if it means walking out of your way a little bit. Jaywalking might seem safe and easy, but it can lead to fines or citations!

Don't: Try to cross between parked cars or at the top of a hill—drivers might not see you if you pop out of nowhere.

Do: Remember what your kindergarten teacher taught you: Look both ways before you cross the street.

Don't: Trust that drivers will see you—they may very well be paying more attention to other cars on the road than to people trying to cross.

WHERE AM I, AND, HEY—WHERE'S EVERYBODY ELSE??

Do: Decide ahead of time on a place to meet, in case anyone gets separated from the group. A famous monument or a specific café are both good options.

Don't: Panic if you get lost or separated from your friends. Take some deep breaths and try to calm down. Freaking out will only make things worse.

Do: Try to call your friends. As a backup, write their phone numbers down on a small piece of paper you can carry with you, just in case you forget your phone. Call from a pay phone if you need to. (It's surprising but true: Pay phones are not yet extinct—and they can be a real lifesaver, too!)

Don't: Wander around the city alone looking for your friends. Wait in a safe and conspicuous place if you don't have a specific destination in mind.

CATCH A SPIDER

Be a hero by fearlessly trapping and releasing spiders
(instead of running away in tears). It's easy,
and no lives need to be harmed in the process!

● ●

1 Wait until the spider is on a wall, window, or other flat surface.

2 Hold a piece of paper in one hand and place a glass over the spider. (And try not to cripple it in the process—after all, spiders are great garden guardians!)

3 With the spider at the bottom of the glass, slip the paper under the rim of the glass, lifting the glass just enough to let the paper get under it.

4 Keep the glass firmly clamped down on the paper and slide your other hand under it.

5 Turn the glass so that the paper is on top and carry it outside. When you're away from the house, put the glass upside down on the ground.

6 Tap the glass so the spider drops onto the paper, then lift up the glass and let it walk away. Everybody's happy, and everybody lives!

LIVE A HACKER-FREE LIFE ONLINE

Going online is totally safe, right? I mean, how can someone steal your money when you're in the privacy of your own home? Well, with today's technology and scams, anyone can steal pretty much anything—including your identity—from anywhere! Beware of viruses, hackers, and sketchy "friends," and keep these tips in mind when you go digital.

● ●

★ Don't open emails or attachments from people you don't know. They may contain viruses.

★ Keep your passwords and usernames secret so that other people can't access your online accounts. (And don't make your passwords really obvious, like your birth date or phone number!)

★ Never give out information such as your home or email address, your real name, age, cell phone number, or school. If a person or unfamiliar website asks you for details about your address, cell phone number, school, or other personal information, close the window and end your session right away. Talk about creepy!

★ Try to keep your online surfing and real world activities separate. And don't accept friend requests from people you don't know. People may not be who they say they are.

WARNING

If someone asks personal questions or is hassling or bullying you, tell a parent, teacher, or even the police. Save any emails or messages as proof.

LOOK AFTER A PLANT

Improve your green thumb and be a friend to foliage by
following these easy tips.

● ●

☆ *Look at the label.* This will tell you if the plant has any special requirements. Cactuses, for instance, do well in sunny window-sills, whereas ferns like more humid environments, which means you ought to sprinkle some water on their leaves every day. Lilies, for their part, like cool conditions, so never leave one in direct sunlight. All this info is usually on the plant's label, so take a peek.

☆ *Water it well.* Only water your plant when the soil feels close to dry. Different types of plants need different amounts of water, but most need more during the spring and summer.

☆ *Check for dead foliage.* Using your fingers, gently pull off any flowers or leaves that have turned brown.

☆ *Dust it.* The leaves of plants can often get dusty and this can stop the plant from growing properly. To help your plant grow big and beautiful, take a damp paper towel and smooth it along the leaves to clean them.

MANAGE YOUR MONEY

Don't waste your hard-earned cash on senseless splurges
that you'll never use. Follow these tips and watch your
pennies grow into big bucks!

● ●

★ *Earn it.* Ask your parents if they'll pay you to do extra chores. Why not offer to wash the car or clean the windows (see Part 4) for some extra money?

★ *Stash it.* Get a box with a lock or a good old-fashioned piggy bank to serve as a personal mini-bank. Save any small change, allowance, or birthday money you get.

★ *Think twice.* If you've got your eye on something you want to buy, think about it for a week before you buy it. If it's still on your mind, you'll know it's worth the splurge (or at least be less likely to regret it later).

★ *Open a bank account.* Ask your parents to help you set up a bank account. This way your money is harder to get hold of, and you probably won't make as many impulse purchases.

PACK A SUITCASE

Do you find packing for vacations or school trips a
real pain? Do you show up with five suitcases, when
everyone else has a small duffel bag? Stop packing
like a Kardashian sister and follow these steps
for some superbly simple suitcase packing.

● ●

1 Before you start to pack, take some time to really think
about where you're going, how long you're staying, and
what you're going to be doing there. Will you need any
special clothes or shoes? And do you *really* need every pair
of shoes that you own?

2 Make a list of everything you want to take with you, and
then lay everything out near your suitcase.

3 Fold bulky items such as jeans and pants in half, and put
these at the bottom of your suitcase. Fold tops and shirts and
layer them on top of the pants.
If space is really tight, you might
want to roll your clothes instead,
which makes them more compact
and has the added benefit of
reducing wrinkles.

4 Roll up underwear and socks
and put them inside your shoes.
These can go around the edges
of your suitcase with the soles
facing out.

> **Tip**
> Going on a
> plane? If you
> check your bag,
> it will go in the hold under
> the plane, so take a smaller
> bag on the plane as a
> carry-on with a toothbrush
> and some clean underwear
> in it, in case your luggage
> goes missing. Be sure to
> check the TSA carry-on rules
> before you go though, since
> there are restrictions when it
> comes to liquids, deodor-
> ants, and even toothpaste.

5 Put anything liquid or breakable, like your toiletries, in a plastic bag. Put this in the middle of the suitcase, cushioned by the clothes for protection.

PREPARE FOR A TEST

Prep like an Ivy Leaguer to reduce your stress and pass your tests with flying colors!

● ●

⭐ Don't cram the night before a test—you just won't be able to take in all the information. Instead, in the week before the test, slowly read through your notes and homework every night. Write key points on some blank sticky notes. Stick them in places where you will come across

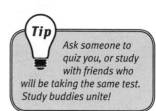

Tip
Ask someone to quiz you, or study with friends who will be taking the same test. Study buddies unite!

them, such as on the fridge or on your bathroom mirror. The more you look at the information, the more you will remember it! Can you say *osmosis*?

⭐ Gather all the items you will need for the test and put them in your backpack the night before to avoid running around looking for them on the day of the test.

⭐ Get a good night's sleep the night before the test so your brain is well rested and ready to go (see Part 2).

⭐ Eat a healthy and substantial breakfast. Good luck!

REMOVE A RING THAT WON'T COME OFF

Did you try on your friend's expensive ring, only to realize
that your knuckles are way bigger than hers? Oops! Before
you panic, follow these simple instructions to remove a
stubbornly stationary ring.

● ●

1 Fill a bowl with cold water and add a whole tray of ice.
Hold the hand with the ring stuck on it in the ice water for
ten seconds.

2 Dry your hand and rub plenty of hand lotion around the ring
and up the length of the finger. (If you don't have any hand
lotion, olive oil or soap work just as well.)

3 Gently twist the ring and slowly work it up and over the
knuckle of your finger. Phew! She never needs to know . . .

TAKE GREAT PHOTOS

You don't need to be Ansel Adams to take great photos.
Whether you just like to shoot pictures of your friends
hanging out or you're more serious about the art, it's easy
to improve the quality of your photos. You don't need
super-expensive camera equipment either—you just need
to adhere to a few simple guidelines.

● ●

★ If you're taking photos of people, avoid busy or distracting
backgrounds. Also look out for random plants or buildings
that could look like they're sticking out of people's heads.

★ When taking pictures of buildings or scenery, most people
take horizontal landscape pictures. Mix it up by trying dra-
matic vertical portraits.

★ Try to get on the same level as the subject of your photo
rather than at an awkward angle looking up their nose or
down at their bald spot.

★ Use the flash, even on sunny days outside. Doing this will fill
in dark, shadowed areas with light.

WRAP A GIFT

Ever give your friend a present that looked like your little brother wrapped it? With his eyes closed? And his hands tied behind his back? Wrap a gift worthy of Santa's elves with these simple steps.

● ●

YOU WILL NEED

• A roll of wrapping paper

• Scissors

• A box big enough to fit your gift inside it

• Tape

• A gift tag

① Unroll some wrapping paper, patterned-side down, onto a clean surface.

② Place the gift inside the box. Place the box upside down in the middle of the paper.

③ Pull the edge of the paper up and over the middle of the box. Then lift the paper up and over from the other side, until it overlaps by about two inches.

④ Cut along the paper in a straight line at this point.

5 Reposition the box in the center of the piece of paper you have just cut.

6 Check that there is enough paper at each of the shorter sides to cover the box, but that there is not too much at each end, otherwise folding it into flaps will be tricky. Trim off any excess paper.

7 Bring the longer edge of paper over to the center of the top of the box and hold it in place with your finger. Then bring the other long edge to the center so that the two edges overlap. Secure it with a piece of tape, as shown.

8 Turn the box over.

9 Position the box so that one of the open ends of the paper is facing you.

10 Fold the sides in as far as you can without tearing the paper. Run your thumb along the edges of the box to make a sharp crease, so that flaps form at the top and bottom, as shown here.

_⑪

⑪ Fold down the top flap of paper and then run your thumb down the sides to make a diagonal crease.

⑫ Place some tape on the center of each flap, then fold them in and secure in place.

⑬ Bring up the bottom flap and secure it with a piece of tape. The end of the box should now be wrapped, as shown here.

⑭ Repeat steps 9 to 13 with the other end of the box.

⑮ Write the name of the person you're giving the gift to on the gift tag in your neatest handwriting and attach it to the top of your wrapped gift. If you're feeling crafty, attach some ribbon or a bow on the top of the box for an extra-special finishing touch!

_⑬

WRITE A GREAT THANK-YOU NOTE

Remember that thing called "mail"? You know, those pieces of paper that come from the place called the "post office"? In a world of emails and text messages, sometimes it's nice to actually mail someone a thank-you note for a gift they gave you. Here are some top letter-writing tips.

● ●

1. On the left-hand side of your paper, write a greeting to the person reading the letter. "What's up!" might be okay for notes to your friends, but remember to keep it appropriate for Grandma.

2. Explain why you are writing. Mention the gift you are thanking them for, say thank you, and tell them why you like it.

3. Add some detail about how you're using the gift or what you're planning to do with it. Even if it was a holiday sweater vest you wouldn't be caught dead in, you can come up with something!

4. Bring in some general information about what you've been doing since you last saw the person you're writing to, to make sure your letter is an interesting read.

5. Repeat your thanks and use an informal way of signing off, such as "Lots of love" or "Looking forward to seeing you soon." Then sign your name and mail it!

Part 2
Looking (and Smelling) Good!

Looks aren't everything in life, but that doesn't mean you shouldn't make an effort! Leave the pajama pants and flip-flops at home, and try going out in style, with some freshly ironed pants, healthy skin, and a bright smile. Now you're looking sharp!

BRUSH BETTER

If you've made it this far in life, you probably know
how to brush your teeth. Maybe you've even flossed
once or twice. But if you're just scraping by with
the basics, it's time to learn how to give your
pearly whites a truly deep clean.

● ●

1 Wet the toothbrush and place a
pea-sized blob of toothpaste on it.

2 Place the toothbrush against your
teeth with the bristles at a forty-
five-degree angle. Move it in
small circles over the outside
of each tooth.

3 Use the same method on the
inside surfaces of your teeth.

4 To gain some leverage on
your hard-to-reach back
teeth, close your mouth slightly
around the toothbrush.

5 Brush the tops of your bottom
back teeth, and the bottoms
of your top back teeth, using
a back and forth motion.

6 And now the key: Don't forget to brush your tongue, too—yes, your tongue—to get rid of bacteria and keep your breath smelling fresh. Some toothbrushes have a tongue-brushing tool on the opposite side of the bristles, but even if your toothbrush is an antique, the bristles can do very well in a pinch.

GET A GOOD NIGHT'S SLEEP

Sick of feeling like a zombie all day? Here's some essential advice to help you get your beauty rest (and avoid being cast in the next postapocalyptic film).

● ●

1 Turn off your TV, computer, and phone at least an hour before you go to bed. Using technology right before you plan to go to sleep can overstimulate your brain and keep you awake.

2 Use your bed only for sleeping in—don't do any last-minute homework under the covers or talk on the phone. This way your brain will think "sleep" as soon as you get into bed.

3 Get your room the right temperature. If it's too hot, you'll toss and turn during the night. Slightly cool is best, because it will make you feel nice and comfortable under the covers.

4 After you turn the lights out, relax by breathing deeply, in and out through your nose, making your *out* breaths last slightly longer than your *in* breaths. This should soon lull you slowly into a deep sleep. *Zzzzz . . .*

Tip

Have a cup of warm milk or chamomile tea half an hour before bedtime. These drinks calm and soothe your body.

IRON A PAIR OF PANTS

Sure, ironing isn't the world's most exciting activity, but let's face it—it *does* look better when your pants are neatly pressed, doesn't it? Stop bugging Mom to iron for you and use these simple steps to do it yourself.

● ●

You Will Need

• An ironing board and iron. If you have a steam iron, make sure you put water in it *before* you plug it in.

1 Set up your ironing board near a wall outlet. Plug in your iron and place it upright on the board.

2 While your iron warms up, check the care label inside the pants. Make sure you set the iron to the appropriate heat level indicated on the label.

3 Once the iron has warmed up, start by ironing the waistband of the pants. Always keep the iron moving, using a sliding motion back and forth. Never, ever leave the iron in place on the pants—this can result in burns and permanent damage.

4 Flip the back pockets of the pants inside out onto the board, and iron them flat.

5 While the pockets are still inside out, iron the back of the pants. Then tuck the pockets back in.

6 Turn the pants over, and do the same with the front pockets and front of the pants. Then tuck the pockets back in.

7 Pull the pants onto the narrow part of the board, as if you were pretending to dress it. This will allow you to iron the front of the pants around the pocket. Do this on both sides.

WARNING

As countless comedy movies and cartoons have shown us, the iron is a very hot object. Always be extra cautious with it, and always remember to unplug it when you're finished.

8 Fold your pants so that the crease will run down the front of your leg. To do this, fold the waist of the pants inward and tuck where the button meets the buttonhole in by about two inches. All of the seams should be on top of one another. Lay the pants folded this way onto the board.

9 Fold the top pant leg up. Gently move the iron over the other pant leg that is still flat on the board.

10 Fold the top pant leg back down, and flip the pants over. Do the same thing on this side.

11 Fold the top leg back down, and iron this side (which should be the outside of the top pant leg).

12 Turn the pants back over, and iron the outside of that leg.

13 Hang the pants immediately, being careful to keep the creases.

14 Turn off and unplug the iron. Put it somewhere safe, where no one will accidently touch it. Who's stylin' now?

POP A PIMPLE

Zits are super gross—but popping one the wrong way can make it look way worse. Keep your acne from approaching def-con level four by following these steps.

● ●

1 Put a mirror in a well-lit area, such as on a windowsill.

2 Wash your hands thoroughly.

3 Does your pimple have a white or black "head" on it? If not, rub some antiacne cream into it and leave it alone. If it does, move onto **step 4**.

4 Wrap each of your index fingers inside a clean tissue, and use these fingers to gently push into the middle of the pimple from either side—this should squeeze out any pus (white or yellow gunk) inside. If nothing comes out, stop squeezing—you don't want to irritate your skin.

5 Clean the zit and the area around it with soap and water, then rub in some antiacne cream.

> **Tip**
> To help keep your skin smooth and pimple-free, eat foods with lots of vitamin C, such as oranges, strawberries, and tomatoes; vitamin E, such as olive oil, sunflower seeds, and hazelnuts; and vitamin A, such as cheese, eggs, and fish. See **Part 3** for help in eating healthfully.

PREVENT SHOE ODOR

Ever wonder why your family runs out of the room as soon
as you take off your shoes? If your smelly sneakers could
knock your friends unconscious, then it's time to get rid of
that odor once and for all! Here's how.

● ●

STOP SMELLS IN THEIR TRACKS

Rule 1. Keep your feet clean by washing them every day. Remember to dry them thoroughly, especially between your toes.

Rule 2. If your sneakers get wet, leave them somewhere airy, such
as the garage, and don't wear them again until they are fully dry.

Rule 3. Wear thick socks made from natural fibers, such as cotton, as these will absorb moisture better than synthetic fabrics.

OPTION 1: BARBECUE IT

⭐ Put some unused lumps of char-
coal from a barbecue bag into a
pair of stockings and tie them at
the top.

⭐ Place one stocking in each shoe
and leave overnight. In the morning you'll enjoy the sweet smell
of success.

OPTION 2: REALLY AP-PEEL-ING

⭐ The next time you eat an orange,
save the peel.

⭐ Place the orange peel inside your shoes and leave overnight.

⭐ Remove the peel the next morning and be amazed by your fresh-smelling footwear!

OPTION 3: BAKING SODA, BABY!

⭐ Steal some baking soda from your kitchen. Put a teaspoonful in each shoe and shake it.

⭐ Leave the baking soda in your shoes overnight. Then shake the powder out in the morning.

⭐ The baking soda will have soaked up the smell overnight, leaving your shoes smelling fresh.

OPTION 4: FRRRREEZING

⭐ Wrap your stinky shoes in a plastic bag and tie the top of the bag into a knot.

⭐ Place the bag in your freezer and leave it overnight.

⭐ The smelly bacteria in your shoes will be destroyed by the icy temperatures, leaving your shoes smelling fresh and clean.

⭐ Don't forget to "thaw" your shoes before you put them on, or your feet will be frozen, too!

SHINE YOUR SHOES

Look spiffy with super-shiny shoes! Here's the best way to polish them to perfection.

● ●

1 Place your shoes on some old newspaper on the floor. (If your shoes have laces, take them out.) Wipe the shoes with a damp cloth to remove any dirt and leave them to dry.

2 Wrap a soft, dry cloth around your index and middle finger. Dip it in some shoe polish—use shoe polish that is the same color as your shoes, or use a clear shoe polish. (And by the way, *never* use polish on suede shoes. Clean them with a stiff brush instead.)

3 Rub the cloth on one shoe in small circular motions, starting from the heel, until the whole shoe is covered in a thin layer of polish. Do the same to the other shoe.

4 Leave the shoes to dry for as long as possible to allow the polish to absorb.

5 Put one hand inside one shoe and, with the other hand, briskly brush all over with a shoe brush. This process is called "buffing" and will make your shoes really shine. Do the same to the other shoe.

6 Repeat **steps 2** to **5** to make your shoes even shinier.

SOAK UP THE SUN (AND AVOID THE BURN)

Unless you've been living under a rock your whole life, you
know that the sun's rays contain harmful UV (ultraviolet)
light that can damage your skin. Still getting burned?
Follow this advice and enjoy the sun without looking like
a lobster and feeling like toast.

● ●

Do: Apply sunscreen about 15 to 20 minutes before you leave
the house to allow it to fully absorb into your skin. Wear a
sunscreen with a sun protection factor (SPF) of at least 30, and
reapply at least every two hours to every part of your body
that is in the sun—don't forget your ears and your toes! Reapply
whenever you've been swimming.

Don't: Stay in the sun too long.
The sun is strongest from 11 a.m. to
3 p.m., so try to stay indoors at these
times. If you are out and about, stay
in the shade whenever possible.

Do: Drink plenty of water while you
are in the sun and after you come inside. This will help you stay
hydrated and stop you from getting sunstroke.

Do: Wear a hat to shade your face and sunglasses with a good
UV rating to protect your eyes, which can be damaged by the
sun, too!

Don't: Be fooled by cloud cover—harmful rays can still get
through and burn your skin even on a cloudy day.

TIE A BOW TIE

You may not wear a bow tie every day, but when the time is right (for instance, when you're saving the world or attending the opera) there's nothing better. (Just ask James Bond.) And you can save yourself a lot of stress by learning how to do it right beforehand, when the countdown clock isn't already ticking.

● ●

1 Stand in front of a mirror with the bow tie around your neck. Leave one side longer than the other by about one and a half inches.

2 Take the longer side and cross it over the other one, then loop it underneath and through.

3 Fold the shorter side, as shown here, with the end at the front.

4 Hold the fold in place with one finger and bring the long side down over it, making a loop.

5 Fold this side, as shown here, with the end at the back.

6 Finally, push this fold through the back of the loop that you made in **step 4**, keeping hold of both ends.

⑥

7 You should now be able to see your bow tie taking shape. For the final shaken-not-stirred look, adjust both ends and tighten your perfect bow tie.

⑦

TIE A TIE

Whether you have to wear a tie to a fancy event or just love to look stylish, follow these easy steps to get all dressed up without getting tied up in knots.

● ●

1 If you're wearing your tie with a shirt, put the collar up, then put the tie around your neck with its narrow end on your right (if you are left-handed, the narrow end should be on your left). Make sure the wide end of the tie hangs down about six inches farther than the narrow end.

2 Take the wide end and bring it over and under the skinny end, so that it is back on the side it started on. The back of the wide end should now be facing out, as shown here.

❸ Bring the wide end back over the top of the narrow end, as shown here.

❹ Push the wide end of the tie through the loop at your neck.

❺ Now push the wide end of the tie down through the loop you have just made.

❻ Tighten the knot by holding onto the narrow end and sliding the knot up to your neck.

WASH YOUR HANDS LIKE A SURGEON

A quick rinse under the faucet won't get your hands germ-free. Here's how to wash them and eliminate lingering germs so your hands will be squeaky clean—even if you aren't performing open heart surgery.

● ●

WHEN TO WASH?

• After going to the bathroom

• Before touching food

• After coughing or sneezing

1 Wet your hands with warm water and lather up (by rubbing soap between your hands for a couple of seconds).

2 Rub your palms together in a circular motion.

3 Rub the back of each hand with the palm of the other hand. Interlace your fingers as you do so.

Tip

You should wash your hands for about twenty seconds—that's about how long it takes to sing the song "Happy Birthday to You" twice. In your head, of course.

4 Place your hands so that the palms are touching and interlace your fingers, as shown here. Rub your hands up and down.

④

5 Bend your fingers so they are curled toward the palm. Link them with the fingers on the other hand and rub together in a circular motion.

6 Hold one thumb and rotate your hand around it.

7 Repeat with your other thumb.

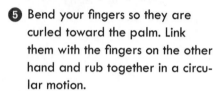
⑤

8 Keeping the fingers on one hand locked together, rotate them around the whole area of the palm of the other hand.

9 Repeat with the other hand.

10 Rinse your hands in warm, running water.

11 Dry thoroughly with a towel. You're good to go!

Part 3
Get to Know Your Kitchen

Do you wait for Mom or Dad to tell you that dinner is ready? Depending on someone else for your meals is bound to leave you very hungry one day. It's time to learn to fend for yourself in the kitchen—with these skills and basic recipes, you can impress your family, friends, and even your date. Get cooking!

EAT A BALANCED MEAL

You may wish you could eat potato chips for every meal (potatoes are a vegetable . . . aren't they?), but having a balanced diet is really important in helping you stay healthy and full of energy. Here's how to eat right every day.

● ●

☆ *The USDA recommends:* About half of your meal should be fruits and vegetables.

☆ *You can eat lots of:* Potatoes, rice, whole-grain pasta, whole-grain breads, and whole-grain noodles.

☆ *You can eat small amounts of:* Cheese, milk, and yogurt.

☆ *Try to cut down on:* Sodas and sugary drinks, chips, candy, cookies, and chocolate.

☆ *Make sure you include some:* Red meat, chicken, eggs, tofu, nuts, and fish.

KITCHEN ESSENTIALS

Before you start whipping up any delicious masterpieces
in the kitchen, you've got to know how to beat bacteria and
deal with potentially dangerous equipment to keep your
cooking clean and safe. Nothing spoils a meal like seeing a
gross kitchen or the chef covered in bloody bandages!

● ●

KEEP IT CLEAN

☆ Before you touch any ingredients, wash your hands well
(see Part 2).

☆ If you're going to be cooking or preparing food, put
bandages on any cuts or scrapes on your hands to
help stop infection.

☆ When you unpack your groceries,
put meat, fish, and dairy products
right into the fridge so they
don't spoil.

☆ Wash your hands thoroughly after
touching raw meat or eggs.

☆ As tempting as it may be, never
eat cake mix or cookie dough
before it's baked—the raw eggs
in batter or dough can make you sick. Save your craving
for cookie dough or brownie batter ice cream!

☆ Wash fruit and vegetables thoroughly before using them.

DON'T GET BURNED

⭐ Always use oven mitts when handling hot plates, pans, or oven doors.

⭐ Turn the handles of hot sauce-pans toward the back of the stove so you won't bump into them. Yow! That's gotta hurt!

⭐ Never lean over electric or gas burners that are switched on.

⭐ Lean back slightly as you pour hot liquids so you don't get scalded by the steam.

⭐ Stand back when opening a hot oven door to avoid the rush of hot air.

⭐ Make sure you've turned off the oven and stove top burners when you're finished cooking.

SHARPEN UP YOUR ACT

⭐ Don't leave sharp knives in the bottom of the kitchen sink, especially if it's full of soapy dishwater. Finding a blade under the bubbles would be a nasty surprise!

★ Pass scissors and knives to people handle-end first, so they don't cut themselves on the blade.

★ Carry knives with the blade pointing downward so that you are safe if you trip. Better to scratch up the floor than your skin.

★ Use cutting boards placed on flat, stable surfaces to prepare ingredients.

SET A TABLE

**Make dinner with your friends extra special by
setting the table restaurant-style!**

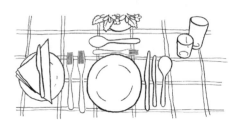

1. Place a fork to the left of the main-course plate. If you are having a starter, such as a salad, place a smaller fork, called a starter fork, to the left of it.

2. Place a knife to the right of the plate. If you are having a starter, place a smaller knife, called a starter knife (do we see a pattern here?) to the right of it. If you are having soup as a starter, place the soup spoon here.

3. Place a dessert spoon horizontally above the top of the plate, with the handle on the right. Place a dessert fork below it, with the handle on the left.

4. Place glasses above and to the right of the knives.

5. Place a side plate to the left of the forks for bread. Fold a napkin in half and place a butter knife on top. Martha Stewart would be impressed.

UNJAM A JAR

The bread's in the toaster, but the lid of your jam jar is stuck. Like, really, totally stuck. And no one is around to help. Try these tricks to get it off.

● ●

⭐ Tap around the edge of the lid with the handle of a wooden spoon. (This will help to knock away whatever's sticking to the lid.)

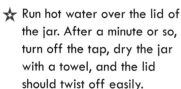

⭐ Slide the tip of the handle of a teaspoon into any gap between the lid and the jar. You may hear a *pop*—this releases air that's holding the lid tight.

⭐ Run hot water over the lid of the jar. After a minute or so, turn off the tap, dry the jar with a towel, and the lid should twist off easily.

⭐ If that still doesn't work, try again but this time while wearing a pair of rubber gloves—they'll give you a tighter grip on the jar.

53

LOAD THE DISHWASHER

Loading the dishwasher is like playing Tetris. It's an art to fit everything properly—and if you can master it, you'll get everything cleaner more quickly! Here's how.

● ●

PRE-PACKING

1 Scrape any excess food from plates or bowls into the garbage.

WARNING

Dishwasher designs may vary. Check your dishwasher's instructions before loading it.

2 Rinse each item under warm water. Why rinse the dishes if you are just going to put them into the dishwasher? Food can clog up your machine, making for a watery mess. It's much easier to remove stray bits of food from your sink strainer than from the bottom of your dishwasher.

3 Check that the items you want to put in the dishwasher are dishwasher safe. Some plastic items may melt and some kinds of silverware can be damaged.

LOAD IT RIGHT

4 Dishwashers are designed so that each item has its own special place. Use the diagram on the facing page to help you locate where things go.

a. Place large and medium-sized plates in the narrow, slotted areas on the bottom rack.

b. Place smaller plates in the narrow, slotted areas on the top rack. Place smaller bowls along the sides of the top rack.

c. Place glasses face down between the spikes on the top rack.

d. Place coffee mugs upside down on the outer edges of the top rack.

e. Place plastic cutting boards along the sides on the bottom rack.

f. Pots and pans should be placed upside down on the bottom rack.

g. Place all cutlery in the removable basket. Always put knives in the dishwasher with the blades pointing down. Don't put large, sharp knives in the dishwasher—wash them by hand instead.

h. Larger utensils should be placed flat on the top rack.

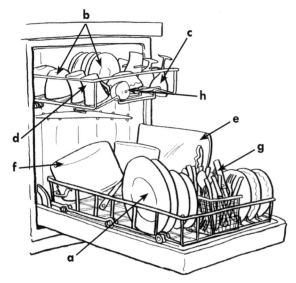

BEFORE YOU TURN IT ON

5 Make sure that there are no big items sticking up that will stop the "washing arm"—found underneath the top rack—from turning. Save some water by only running the dishwasher when it's full.

6 Place the dishwasher tablet, powder, or liquid in the space provided—usually inside a flap on the inside of the door.

7 Push the door shut and choose the Wash setting (Quick Wash, Normal, and so on).

8 After the washing cycle is done, wait a few minutes to give the dishes time to cool down before you unload them. Unload the bottom level first, as water may drip from items above.

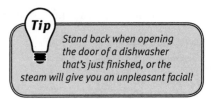

Tip
Stand back when opening the door of a dishwasher that's just finished, or the steam will give you an unpleasant facial!

PEEL POTATOES

If you want to enjoy any potatoey treats (besides the old baked potato, of course), you're going to have to master the art of potato peeling. Here's how.

● ●

1 Hold the potato in your left hand if you're right-handed, or in your right hand if you're left-handed.

2 Hold the peeler firmly in your other hand. Position the blade so that it is on the top of the potato.

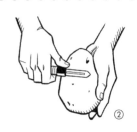

3 Push the peeler down and stroke it away from you. Peel the rest of the top half of the potato in this way.

4 Turn the potato around and peel the other half in the same way.

5 Turn the potato over and repeat **steps 3** and **4** on the ends.

6 Rinse the potato with cold water and throw away the peelings. Eek! It's a naked potato!

WARNING

Potato peelers can be deceptively sharp, so watch out!

CHOP GARLIC

Whether you're warding off vampires or adding some flavor to your Superlative Pasta (see page 66), garlic is an essential ingredient. Learn to chop garlic like an Iron Chef with these simple steps.

● ●

1 Peel the skin off the head of garlic to expose the clove you want to use.

2 Pull off the clove you need.

3 Place the clove down lengthwise on a cutting board.

4 Place the flat part of a chef's knife across the clove. Using your fist, carefully smash the blade. Don't Hulk out too much, though—you don't want to nick yourself on the sharp edge!

④

5 This should loosen the skin on the clove. Using your fingers, peel the skin off and discard it in the garbage or compost pile. It might stick a little, so be patient.

?

Did you know...

A head of garlic is the bulbous-looking root you buy at the store. A clove of garlic is one piece of the head.

6 With your knife, carefully cut off the flat bottom part of the clove and toss it in the garbage or compost pile.

7 Once you have the fully exposed clove of garlic, cut it lengthwise into small strips. Chop the strips into smaller pieces, and voilà!

Tip

The smell of the garlic tends to linger on your fingers for a long time, even after washing your hands. To get rid of the smell, you can try using a lemon fragrance soap that says it fights odors, rubbing your fingers with a silver spoon (if you have a silver spoon, you fancy chef), or using rubber gloves when you are doing your chopping.

CHOP AN ONION

Chop an onion like a master chef using this crafty technique.

● ●

1 Place the onion on its side on a cutting board. If you're right-handed, the root should be on the left-hand side and the top on the right, as shown here. If you're left-handed, turn the onion so that the root end is on your right.

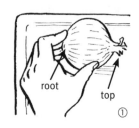

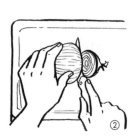

2 Using a sharp knife, slice off the top of the onion.

3 Peel off the crispy outer layer of skin and throw it away.

⚠️

WARNING

It's obvious but still worth repeating: Knives are meant for cutting, so pay attention and make sure you cut the things you want (and not the things you don't, like your hand).

4 Cut the onion in half down the middle, from the top to the root.

5 Place one onion half, with the cut side face down, on the cutting board.

6 With the knife pointing toward the root, hold the onion with your other hand and carefully slice downward, starting from the root end and finishing at the top end to make a series of horizontal cuts. Repeat until all the onion is sliced.

7 Using your fingers to hold the sliced sections together, turn the knife and slice all the way across the onion, to make a series of vertical cuts until you reach the root. Throw away the root.

8 Repeat **steps 5** to **7** with the other onion half.

CRACK AN EGG

Fear the shell no more—cracking eggs looks tricky, but it's really just a case of cracking the steps below.

● ●

1 Gently tap the egg on the side of a bowl to make a small indent in the shell.

2 Holding the egg with the fingers of both hands over the bowl, push into the indent with your thumbs.

3 Once your thumbs have broken through the shell, pry the shell apart, so that the contents of the egg fall into the bowl.

SEPARATING THE WHITE FROM THE YOLK

For some recipes, you need just the yolk or just the white part of the egg. Read on to find out how to separate the two.

1 Crack the egg, and then pour the contents from one half of the shell to the other (instead of into the bowl), keeping the yolk intact but letting the white drip down into the bowl.

2 Transfer the yolk from shell to shell until all of the white part has fallen into the bowl and the yolk is left in the shell.

UPGRADE YOUR SKILLS TO PROFESSIONAL STATUS BY MASTERING THE ONE-HANDED EGG BREAK (Next Food Network Star, anyone?)

1 Hold the egg in your stronger hand, with your thumb on one side, your index finger hooked over the top of the egg, and your middle and ring fingers on the other side.

2 Tap the egg firmly against the rim of the bowl or cup.

3 Place your middle finger over the crack and pull the front of the shell upward. At the same time, use your thumb to push gently against the eggshell to move the two halves in opposite directions.

4 As the egg pours into the bowl or cup, raise your hand briskly. Ta-da!

> ⚠️
> **WARNING**
> *Wash your hands thoroughly after handling raw eggs (see Part 2). Germs!*

BOIL AN EGG

What's not to like about boiled eggs? They're super-tasty,
super-filling, and super-healthy—and yes, even you
can make them. Make a whole batch of boiled eggs
so you can enjoy them during the week. Sounds like
an *egg-cellent* idea, doesn't it?

● ●

TO MAKE SOFT-BOILED EGGS

1 Take your egg out of the fridge about an hour before you
want to cook it. Very cold eggs may crack when they touch
hot water.

2 Make a tiny pinprick in the shell
at the fattest end of the egg to
let steam escape while the egg
cooks.

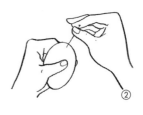

3 Pour water into a saucepan—
enough to cover the whole egg
by roughly half an inch.

4 Heat the water so that it is gently simmering. You can recognize
a good simmer by the teeny
bubbles climbing up the sides of
the saucepan.

5 Slowly lower the egg into the
water with a spoon.

6 Cook the egg for four minutes if you want a soft, runny yolk. If you like a firmer yolk, cook for six minutes instead.

7 Turn the stove off; then remove the egg from the pan with the spoon and place it in an eggcup.

8 Slice away the top of the eggshell using the edge of a teaspoon to reveal the yummy yolk inside. Why not serve with hot, buttered toast?

TO MAKE HARD-BOILED EGGS

1 Repeat **steps 1** to **5** on the opposite page.

2 Cook the egg for seven minutes, then turn the stove off.

3 Remove the egg from the pan with a spoon and hold it under cold, running water to cool it down, then leave it in a bowl of cold water for two minutes.

4 Peel away the shell of the egg. Cut the egg into quarters, and serve with a fresh, crispy salad for an *eggs-traordinarily* tasty lunch! Okay, okay—enough with the puns.

⚠ WARNING

Stay alert when you're boiling water on the stove. Nobody likes boiled fingers.

COOK SUPERLATIVE PASTA

Cooking pasta may seem easy, but the art of cooking great pasta—pasta that doesn't crunch when you bite into it or disintegrate in the pot—requires some attention to detail.

● ●

1 Fill a large pot with cold water. Turn on the heat and wait until the water is boiling.

2 Add a large pinch of salt to the water for flavor, and add a splash of olive oil—this will stop the pasta from sticking to the pot.

3 Carefully add the pasta to the pan. You should allow two ounces of uncooked pasta for each adult (or about one cup of cooked pasta). Pasta expands as it cooks, so avoid the rookie mistake of cooking the whole box for two people. Push the pasta down with a wooden spoon until the water covers it.

4 Check the cooking instructions on the pasta box and set a timer accordingly—generally nine to ten minutes is a good cooking time, but it always depends on what kind of pasta you are using.

5 While the pasta is cooking, stir it several times to make sure it doesn't stick to the bottom of the pan.

6 After the timer has gone off, use a fork to fish out a piece of pasta to taste. Perfectly cooked pasta should be "al dente," which means it's soft enough to eat, but is still firm when you bite into it. If you like your pasta softer, just cook it for a minute or two more.

7 Place a colander in the sink and, using oven mitts, take the pot off the stove and pour the pasta and water into it to drain.

Tip

Try pepping up your finished pasta with . . .

- *butter and black pepper.*
- *basil leaves and tomatoes.*
- *sauce and grated Parmesan.*

CREATE AN OMELET

Sick of eating cereal for breakfast every morning? Omelets are an excellent source of protein, and with cheese and veggies, an omelet makes a very well-balanced meal. Get in touch with your inner Julia Child with this easy recipe!

●●●●●●●●●●●●●●●●●●●●●●●●●●●●●●●●●

You will need:

- 2 eggs
- Salt and pepper to taste
- ½ cup chopped broccoli
- ½ cup sliced mushrooms
- 1 tbsp. butter
- Cheese of your choice

This recipe serves one person.

1 Crack the eggs into a bowl. Add the salt and pepper (just a pinch of each). With a wire whisk or fork, whisk the eggs until they are fully beaten.

2 Prep your other ingredients—chop the broccoli if it isn't chopped already, and slice up the mushrooms if they are still whole.

3 Place a skillet onto the burner and turn the burner on to medium heat.

4 Put the butter in the skillet and allow it to melt. Use a spatula to spread the butter around the pan as it melts.

5 Pour the eggs into the skillet.

6 Allow the eggs to cook for several minutes, until they are no longer runny. To make sure they don't stick to the pan, move the eggs with your spatula every so often.

7 Once the eggs are just about cooked, sprinkle the desired amount of cheese over the omelet.

8 Add in the broccoli and mushrooms to one side of the omelet, and allow them to cook on the eggs for a few minutes.

9 Using your spatula, take the side of the omelet that doesn't have the veggies on it, and fold it over the side that does.

10 Carefully flip the omelet over, so that the side you just put on top is now on the bottom.

11 Give it another minute or two to cook the veggies until they are cooked to your liking (longer if you want them softer). Then place your omelet on a plate, and bon appétit!

> **Tip**
>
> The beauty of an omelet is that you can fill it with just about anything you want—tomatoes, basil, asparagus, broccoli, spinach, peppers, ham, even beans and salsa! The recipe here is just an example, so experiment by adding your favorite fillings!

MAKE YOUR OWN TRAIL MIX

Trail mix isn't just for hippies and earthy-crunchy environmentalists. It's a tasty, nutritious snack that you can easily grab on the go, whether you are hitting the trails or heading to school.

● ●

You will need:

- 3 cups of granola
- 1 cup of raisins
- 1 cup of dried cranberries
- 1 cup of banana chips
- ½ cup of dark chocolate chunks
- 1 cup of shelled nuts, such as peanuts, almonds, or walnuts

Mix all these ingredients together in a bowl. Store in an airtight container, or separate into baggies so you can grab one on the run!

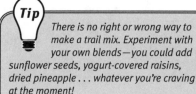

Tip

There is no right or wrong way to make a trail mix. Experiment with your own blends—you could add sunflower seeds, yogurt-covered raisins, dried pineapple . . . whatever you're craving at the moment!

MAKE A SMOOTHIE

Smoothies are delicious and super-healthy. Read on to find out how to become a smoothie operator.

● ●

You will need:

- 1 ripe banana, cut in half
- 1 small glass of milk
- 1 small container of plain yogurt
- 1 small bag of frozen berries
- 1 tsp. honey

WARNING

Be careful when using a blender— make sure you always keep the lid on while it's running, unless you are thinking of repainting your kitchen walls!

This recipe serves two people.

1 Put all the ingredients together in a blender.

2 Make sure the lid of the blender is firmly in place, then switch the blender on.

3 Blend until the mixture is smooth and there are no big lumps of fruit.

4 Split between two glasses and serve. Fruity and delicious!

②

Tip

Why not make your own signature smoothie by experimenting with lots of different ingredients? Try using ice cream instead of yogurt for a deliciously creamy smoothie.

PREPARE PERFECT PANCAKES

Pancakes are delicious whether you're having them for weekend brunch or you're indulging in a little breakfast for dinner. Follow these steps to make and flip a perfect pancake.

● ●

You will need:

- 2 cups all-purpose flour
- 2 tbsp. sugar
- 3 tsp. baking powder
- 1 egg
- 2 tbsp. oil
- 1½ cups milk
- 2 tbsp. unsalted butter

This recipe makes twelve to fourteen pancakes.

1 Sift the flour, sugar, and baking powder into a large mixing bowl.

2 Make a small hollow in the flour and break the egg into it.

3 Mix the egg and flour together with a whisk or a fork.

4 In another bowl, mix the oil and the milk together.

5 Gradually pour the milk mixture into the bowl, whisking all the time. You should now have a smooth batter with no lumps of flour.

6 Melt the butter in a frying pan. (This frying pan will be used to cook and flip your pancakes, so make sure it's not too heavy.)

7 Turn the heat up under the pan, and spoon a ladleful of the batter into the center.

8 Let the batter cook until bubbles start to form on the surface.

⑦

9 Shake the pan from side to side to check that the pancake is not sticking. You may need to gently slide a spatula underneath to get it sliding around properly.

10 Grip the handle of the pan with both hands and lift it off the burner.

11 Flick the pan upward in a smooth, scooping motion so that the pancake flips up and all the way over.

⑪

12 Let the pancake cook for one minute on the other side. Then serve with your favorite toppings!

Tip

If your flipping attempt fails, use a wide metal spatula to turn the pancake over.

SERVE TRANSCENDENT TEA

A perfect cup of tea on a cold winter's day is sure to put a smile on anyone's face. Here's how to make tea the British would be proud of.

● ●

1 Fill your kettle with fresh cold water; then boil on the stove.

2 Line up the mugs or teacups, tea-pot, spoons, and sugar. Leave the milk in the fridge until later.

3 Pour some warm water from the tap into the teapot. Carefully swirl the water around for thirty seconds then pour it away. A warm pot will help the tea release its color and flavor.

4 Put spoonfuls of loose tea or tea bags into the pot—one spoonful or tea bag for each person and one extra.

5 After the kettle has boiled, pour the water into the pot. Pour slowly and be careful not to scald yourself in the steam.

6 Stir the tea in the pot, then leave it to brew for three min-utes—any longer than that and the tea will start to taste bitter.

7 Pour a splash of chilled milk into the mugs or teacups, then pour in the tea. If you have used loose tea, you will need to hold a strainer over the top of each mug or cup as you pour, to catch the tea leaves.

8 If your guests want sugar, stir it in thoroughly for them and serve. Mind your pinkies!

Part 4
Clean Up Like a Pro (and Maybe Earn Some Extra Dough)

Cleaning may not be anyone's favorite activity, but keeping things clean and tidy makes life way easier (and prettier!). As an added bonus, you can earn some extra cash from your parents and neighbors by offering to clean windows, rake leaves, and wash cars—for a price! Use the tips in this chapter to help beautify and organize your life.

CLEAN WINDOWS

Cleaning windows doesn't take a ton of time and makes
a big impact. Here's how to get that glass looking
so clear, even the birds will be confused.

● ●

1 Pick a cloudy day to wash the windows—sunshine will dry them too quickly, leaving streaks on the glass.

WARNING

Stick to low windows you can easily reach. Leave the higher and hard-to-reach spots to the professionals with ladders.

2 Put on rubber gloves and fill a bucket halfway with warm water. Add several splashes of white vinegar and mix well.

3 Start by washing the outside of the windows. Soak a cloth or sponge in the water and rub the window side to side, and then up and down.

4 Use a squeegee—a tool with a rubber blade—to wipe away any excess water. Wipe down the window in a zigzag movement from side to side.

5 Use a soft, clean cloth to dry the glass and make it shine. Rub the cloth all over the window in circular movements.

6 Repeat **steps 3** to **5** on the inside.

Tip

Before cleaning the windows, lay down sheets of newspaper to catch any drips.

CLEAN YOUR ROOM IN FIVE MINUTES

Parents on your case about cleaning up your room? Don't worry—it shouldn't take more than five minutes to tidy up. Start the clock!

● ●

⭐ *Five minutes to go.* Put any dirty clothes into the laundry basket. Hang clean clothes in your closet or fold them and put them in your dresser.

⭐ *Four minutes to go.* Get rid of the clutter! Put any school papers on your desk in a neat pile and pop all your stationery in a desk drawer. Get a garbage bag and scan the room for anything that can be thrown away. Do you really need that empty shoe box that has been sitting on your floor since last Christmas? Toss it!

⭐ *Three minutes to go.* Collect all your books, DVDs, and games and organize them on shelves in height order so that they look tidy. Place any jewelry and accessories in neat little boxes.

★ ***Two minutes to go.*** Pick up any dirty plates, cups, or bowls and take them to the kitchen to clean later. How long have those been sitting there, anyway?

★ ***One minute to go.*** Shake out your duvet or comforter, then smooth it down and fluff up the pillows. Prepare for your parents to be shocked!

Tip

If you're willing to spend the extra few minutes, vacuum your carpet. There's something magical about a freshly vacuumed carpet that makes a room look extra clean!

DO THE LAUNDRY

Doing laundry takes some real skill—get it wrong and your best white shirt will come out as a pink crop top. Follow this guide and take the worry out of doing the washing.

• •

1 Separate all the dirty clothes into the following piles.

- Whites—Go through this pile carefully to check that there are no stray dark socks.

- Colors—Include pastel-colored or bright clothes.

- Darks—Include black or navy items and dark jeans.

2 Check that all pockets are empty. Hard items such as keys will damage the washing machine and stray tissues will leave tiny pieces of fluff all over your clothes. And you don't even want to know what gum will do to both your clothes and the machine!

3 Find the care label and read the washing instructions on it. The label is usually inside the garment, stitched into a seam, and it should tell you the temperature of water that the garment needs (cold, warm, or hot), or if it should be dry-cleaned or hand-washed.

4 Separate the garments within each pile into groups that should be washed at the same temperature, keeping them sorted by color.

5 Place the first load of laundry into the machine and close the door.

6 Open the detergent drawer and fill the correct section with a scoop of powder detergent or cap of liquid laundry detergent. If you use tablets, pop these directly inside the machine.

7 Pour a cap of fabric softener into the specified section of the drawer and close it.

8 Select the correct setting on the washing machine for the load you are washing and press Start. Now it's the washing machine's turn to do some work!

Tip

Washing clothes at a lower temperature than indicated on the care label won't harm them. But never wash them at a higher temperature, unless you want your clothes to fit Barbie!

FOLD A FITTED SHEET

Create order from chaos in your linen closet by learning to fold a fitted sheet. Sure, it has round edges, elastic seams, and generally looks like an ill-shaped parachute, but it's actually pretty easy if you follow these steps.

● ●

1 While standing up, hold the fitted sheet vertically with the side you sleep on facing you. Place each hand in one of the top corners as if you are slipping on a pair of mittens, with your arms wide open.

2 Bringing one hand to the other hand, tuck one corner into the other corner.

3 While still holding that corner from the inside with one hand, slide your free hand down to the other corners. Do the same thing—tuck one corner into the other. You may need to do some finagling here, using your covered hand to help guide the corners, or ask someone to help you out. Now you should have a long rectangular shape, with the two tucked corners in each hand.

4 Take the corners in your right hand and tuck them into the corners in your left hand. Now you should have a sort of square.

5 Place the square on a flat service, and make sure everything is tucked neatly. Fold the sheet in half, and then fold it in half again. Amazing!

PUT ON A DUVET COVER

Putting on a duvet cover doesn't have to be a wrestling match. Turn yourself into a duvet master with this easy-to-follow guide.

● ●

❶ Flatten out your comforter on the bed, then turn your clean duvet cover inside out and lay it flat over the duvet, making sure the fastenings are undone.

❷ Put your arms inside the cover until you reach the corners of the duvet cover that are farthest away.

❸ Grab the top corners of the comforter while keeping your hands inside the cover, then shake the cover down over it, so the cover is now right-side out.

❹ Push the other two corners of the comforter into the bottom corners of the duvet cover.

❺ Close the fastenings and give the whole thing a final big shake or two, before smoothing it over your bed. Perfection!

PUT YOUR CLOTHES AWAY

Have your clothes abandoned the closet for a wrinkly pile
on the floor? Does it take a ten-minute search to find socks
that actually match? Follow these simple folding tips to
keep your clean clothes organized and uncrumpled.

● ●

TIP-TOP TOPS AND T-SHIRTS

❶ Turn T-shirts, polo shirts, and sweaters face down on a
flat surface.

❷ Take one sleeve and fold it over
from the shoulder seam so that
the sleeve is pointing downward,
as shown.

❸ Repeat **step 2** with the other
sleeve.

❹ Pick up the top and fold it in
half, with the sleeves on the inside, so it's roughly rectangular.
Then place it in a drawer.

BE A "JEAN"-IUS

❶ Flatten out jeans and other
pants and lay them out on a
flat surface. Fold them in half
lengthways with one leg on top
of the other, as shown here.

2 Fold the jeans or pants in half so that the waistband and hem of the leg are touching, and hang them over a coat hanger in your closet.

GET SHIRT SMART

1 Hang clean shirts on coat hangers, using one shirt per hanger, and smooth them down to make sure there are no wrinkles.

2 Button one or two buttons to keep the shirts on the hangers. Hang them in your closet.

SOCK IT TO 'EM

1 Sort through clean socks and find all the matching pairs.

2 Take a matching pair, hold the tops of the socks together, and roll one over the other, forming a ball that will keep them together.

3 Keep all your paired up socks together in a drawer.

RAKE THE LEAVES

If your yard is in danger of disappearing under a
carpet of autumn leaves, save it from extinction
with this super-efficient way to rake.

● ●

1 Put on a long-sleeved shirt or sweat-
shirt, old jeans, and a pair of gar-
dening gloves. These will protect you
from any thorns or sharp stones that
may be hidden among the leaves.

2 Using a wide, fan-shaped rake, drag
the tines of the rake over the leaves
on the lawn, making short strokes
toward you, to create a small pile of leaves.

3 Lay an old sheet flat on the lawn beside the pile of leaves.
Sweep the leaves onto the sheet using the rake.

4 Carefully, pick up all four corners of the sheet, keeping the
leaves safely stowed in the middle of the sheet, and carry
the bundle to the compost bin. If you don't have a compost
bin, fill garbage bags with the leaves and put them out for
the garbage truck to collect.

5 Repeat **steps 2** to **4** until all the leaves have been cleared
from the lawn.

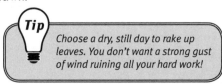

Tip

*Choose a dry, still day to rake up
leaves. You don't want a strong gust
of wind ruining all your hard work!*

REMOVE A STAIN

Just because you spilled something all down your
front doesn't mean that your favorite shirt is a goner.
Here's how to get rid of stains.

● ●

STAIN: CHOCOLATE

Put the stained clothing in a plastic
bag in the freezer until the chocolate
has hardened, then scrape off the
chocolate with a butter knife. Run the
remaining stain under hot water and
massage in a little laundry detergent.
Wash the garment as normal.

STAIN: INK

If the stain is on colored fabric, soak
it in a bowl of warm milk for a few
minutes, then wash the garment as
normal. If the stain is on white fabric,
cover the stain with salt, then rub it
with lemon juice and wash normally.

STAIN: GLUE

Pour a small amount of nail polish
remover onto a cotton ball and dab
away at the stain; then wash the
garment as normal.

STAIN: TEA OR COFFEE

Rinse the stain under cold water. Rub some liquid laundry detergent directly onto the stain, massaging it into the fabric. Continue massaging firmly for a minute, then rinse and wash as normal. Never use hand or dish soap, as this will "set" the stain.

UNSTICK CHEWING GUM

So, in one of your rare rebel-without-a-cause moments,
you spit your gum out nonchalantly, only to have it land
(and stick) on your shirt. Not feeling so cool now, right?
Don't worry—here's how to remove it.

● ●

1 Put the gum-afflicted item into the freezer and leave it
there overnight.

2 In the morning, remove the item
and take it to the sink. Use a butter knife to carefully scrape off
the frozen gum.

3 Use a clean cloth soaked in
water and a squirt of dish soap
to wipe away any traces of the
gum. Leave the item to dry completely, then wash as normal.

Tip

*To get chewing gum out of your hair, hold an
ice cube over the affected area. When the gum
hardens, pick it off with your fingers. Remove
any remaining bits of gum by massaging peanut butter
into the hair. Then comb the area using a fine-toothed
comb. And stop recklessly spitting out your gum!*

WASH A CAR

When you're looking for a little extra cash, why not
offer to wash the car? It's the perfect summer-day activity!
Your neighbors might jump in line to have their cars
cleaned, too. Here's how to do it.

● ●

You will need:

- A hose (optional)
- Two buckets
- Car wash soap
- Rubber gloves
- A sponge
- A stiff brush
- A chamois leather
  (or a clean, soft
  cloth)
- Two clean, dry cloths
- Car wax

Tip

For an extra-special clean, finish the job by vacuuming the seats and the floor inside the car.

1 Loosen the top layer of grime by hosing the car down or
pouring buckets of cold water over it.

2 Fill one of the buckets with a mixture of warm water and car
wash soap, and the other with clean, cold water.

3 Wearing rubber gloves, dip the sponge into the warm, soapy
water. Start by cleaning the roof; then work your way down the
body of the car, moving your sponge in big, circular movements.

4 Don't forget to clean the bumpers, wheel arches, and underneath the windshield wipers.

5 The wheels are usually the dirtiest part of the car, so wash them last. Use the brush to get rid of any stubborn dirt, but do not use the brush on the paintwork, as it may cause damage.

⑤

6 Every time the sponge gets dirty, dip it in the bucket of cold water to rinse it. Change the water in the bucket when it gets too grimy.

7 Rinse off all the soap with the hose, or a bucket of clean, cold water.

⑦

8 Dry the car's paintwork with the chamois leather.

9 Dab one of the clean, dry cloths into the car wax and work it slowly into the paintwork in little circular motions. The wax will make the paintwork look cloudy. Use the other clean, soft cloth to rub the wax until the car shines. Wax on, wax off!

Tip
It is really worth investing in car wash soap, because household soaps and detergents can strip the car's finish.

Part 5
Do It Yourself

You might be tempted to pawn off tricky tasks, such as sewing or tying complicated knots, on someone else. But, with a little instruction and training, these tasks can be totally DIY! Be your own handyman (or handy-mam) and learn how to mend, patch, and sew.

FIX A FLAT

If your bike's got a flat tire and no amount of pumping is keeping it up, it might have a puncture. Before you lug your bike to the bike shop, follow these steps to find out how to fix the flat tire yourself.

● ●

You will need:

- A cup of water
- Your owner's manual
- A puncture repair kit containing rubber patches, glue, and sandpaper
- Tire levers (optional)
- A bucket of water
- A cloth
- Chalk or a crayon
- A bike pump

Tip

To help you identify all of the parts mentioned in this skill, refer to the diagram of a bike wheel on page 98.

❶ First, you need to check the cause of the flat tire—it might not actually be a puncture, but just the result of a leaky valve. To test the valve, unscrew the dust cap on the flat tire, and hold a cup of water under the valve, so that the valve is completely underwater. If you see bubbles in the water, this means you have a leaky valve, not a punctured tire, and you'll need to take your bike to a bike repair shop. No bubbles? Then continue to **step 2**.

tire valve

2 Inspect all around the tire. Can you see any sharp items that may have caused the puncture? If so, carefully remove any obvious puncture causes, such as nails or thorns, wrap in a tissue, and throw away, then continue to **step 3**.

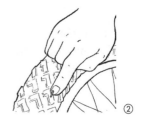
②

3 Disengage (which means unfasten) the brakes. Your owner's manual should tell you how to do this.

4 Next, unscrew the tire valve (or press a button on it depending on the type of valve your bike has) to let any remaining air out of the inner tube—this is the tube that sits inside the tire.

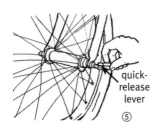

quick-release lever

⑤

5 Remove the wheel by opening the quick-release mechanism that holds the wheel to the frame. To do this, pull the lever outward, as shown on the left. (If your bike does not have a quick-release lever, refer to the owner's manual to find out how to remove the wheel.)

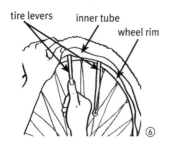

tire levers   inner tube

wheel rim

⑥

6 Carefully pull the inner tube out from inside the wheel rim. You can use tire levers to help pry it out if you have them.

7 Push the valve through the hole in the rim as well. (You may need to unscrew it first, depending on your bike.)

8 To find the puncture hole, listen along the length of the inner tube for a hiss of escaping air, or hold it next to your cheek and feel for a rush of air. If you can't find the puncture hole, place sections of the inner tube into the bucket of water. Bubbles should come out of the place where the hole is in the tube.

9 Dry off the inner tube with the cloth, and mark the area of the hole with chalk so you can find it again.

10 Roughen the rubber around the puncture hole using the sandpaper from your puncture repair kit.

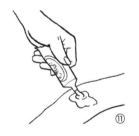

11 Spread a blob of glue over the hole, then leave it for a few moments until it feels "tacky" to the touch.

12 Take the patch from your puncture repair kit and squeeze a tiny blob of glue on the contact surface of the patch. Again, wait until it goes tacky.

13 Apply the patch over the puncture hole. Hold the patch on firmly for two minutes to set it in place. Smooth it down to remove any air bubbles.

14 Carefully peel away the backing sheet on the patch.

15 Dust the inner tube with chalk, especially all around the puncture patch. This stops the tube from sticking to the inside of the tire.

⑭

16 Pull the tire away from the rim and look inside for any glass or nails. Remove any items carefully. Wrap them in a tissue and throw the tissue away.

17 Pump up the inner tube slightly—this will make it easier to fit back on the rim of the wheel.

18 Push part of the inner tube back over the wheel rim. Make sure that the valve is aligned with the hole in the wheel rim and carefully slot it back through. Make sure that it points down toward the hub.

19 Tuck the rest of the inner tube over the rim of the wheel, underneath the tire.

20 Use the bike pump to inflate the tire until it is firm to touch.

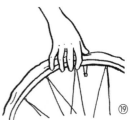
⑲

21 Reattach the wheel to your bike by positioning it between the brake pads and closing the quick-release mechanism, if you have one.

22 Reengage the brakes—refer to your owner's manual to find out how to do this—and test that they're in working order before riding off.

INFLATE YOUR BIKE TIRES

Even without a puncture, bicycle tires lose air and need to be pumped up every so often. Follow these steps and you'll have your tires ready to go again in no time.

● ●

GET PUMPING

1 Lean your bike against a wall, or balance it on its stand.

2 Find the valve and remove the dust cap (use the diagram on the next page to help you locate it). Once you've unscrewed it, put it somewhere safe, like your back pocket.

②

3 Push your bike pump on to the valve stem and secure it. There are different types of bike pumps— some models screw on to the valve, while others use a clamp lever. Read the manual for your pump to find out how yours works.

③

4 Start pumping with a push-and-pull action, and keep going until your bike tire is firm to the touch. Be careful not to over-inflate the tire.

> **Tip**
>
> *Make sure you check your tires regularly. If you find that they keep going flat, you may have something called a slow puncture, which will need to be patched.*

⑤ Take the pump off the valve and screw the dust cap back on.

⑥ Repeat **steps 2** to **5** on the other tire.

"Wheely" Important Info

If you ride your bike often, the air pressure in your tires will gradually decrease. Eventually you might end up with a sad-looking flat tire, which is dangerous to cycle with. To help you get back on the road quickly, look at the diagram below, and learn the names of all the different parts of a bike wheel. This will also come in handy when you need to fix a puncture.

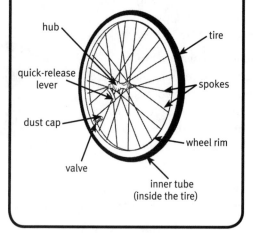

hub

tire

quick-release lever

spokes

dust cap

wheel rim

valve

inner tube (inside the tire)

MEND A SEAM

You've just discovered a giant hole in the side
of your favorite shirt. What can you do?! There's no
need to throw it out yet—if the tear is along a
seam, it's pretty easy to fix. Here's how.

●●●●●●●●●●●●●●●●●●●●●●●●●●●●●

1 Turn your shirt inside out and find the rip in the seam.

2 Carefully pin the two edges of
the seam flat against each other.

3 Turn the shirt right side out to
make sure the join looks okay,
and adjust if necessary.

4 Thread your needle with thread
that matches the stitching in
your shirt.

5 Working on the inside of the
shirt, start stitching just before
the start of the rip. Push the
needle down through the exist-
ing seam, and weave it back
up again, pulling the thread
through. Secure the end of
your thread by making a few
small stitches in one place.

6 Continue this down-and-up motion along the length of the rip.
This is called a running stitch. Be careful not to pull the thread
too tight, or the fabric will bunch.

7 To make sure your stitches are really secure, you need to do something called overstitching. Here's how to do it. From the point where you finished your running stitch, insert the needle through one side of the seam, and push it straight out the other side. Loop the thread over the seam and reinsert the needle on the same side as before, a little farther down. Continue in this way back along the length of your running stitches.

⑦

8 To finish, sew three or four small stitches over the top of one another.

⑨

9 Pull the thread tight and snip it off, then turn the shirt right-side out and admire your sewing skills.

PITCH A TENT

There are many things to love about the great outdoors: fresh air, beautiful scenery, wildlife . . . But one thing that nature doesn't provide is a cozy place to sleep. Before you set out into the great outdoors, you need to know how to pitch a tent. Be extra prepared and practice in your backyard before you go. Remember, every tent is different, so keep your tent's assembly instructions with you.

● ●

1 Choose your spot. Look for somewhere flat, clear of roots and rocks and with no signs of animal tracks or nests—unless you want to get snuggly with a family of raccoons. Try not to pitch on very low ground or near water, in case of flooding.

2 Lay out the tent parts and instructions near your chosen location and check that nothing is missing.

3 If your tent has a groundsheet, stretch this out flat on the ground.

4 Lay the tent flat over the top of the groundsheet and make sure that the entrance is zipped shut.

5 Assemble all the metal supporting poles your tent needs and place them in position. For many tents, this will mean placing the two poles diagonally from corner to corner, and pushing them carefully through the seams in the fabric of the tent.

6 Push the ends of the poles through the loops at the corners of your tent (called grommets), and carefully bend the poles into arches.

7 If your tent has clips, attach these to the arched poles. Your tent should now be taking shape.

8 Put pegs into the grommets at each of the four corners of your tent and push them into the ground at a forty-five-degree angle. You may need to use a mallet to hammer them in if the ground is hard.

9 To waterproof and further secure your tent, place the rain cover (also called the fly sheet) over the top of your tent. Make sure that the door of the fly sheet is aligned with the door of the inner tent so you can get in and out.

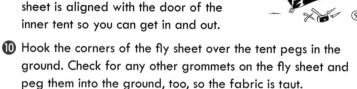

10 Hook the corners of the fly sheet over the tent pegs in the ground. Check for any other grommets on the fly sheet and peg them into the ground, too, so the fabric is taut.

11 Finally, for extra security, pull the ropes on the fly sheet until they are taut, and peg them into the ground.

SEW ON A BUTTON

If a button comes loose from your favorite coat, don't panic—
follow the steps below to learn how to sew it back on.

● ●

1 Thread a needle with about twenty inches of thread in a color that matches your button. Pull the needle down to the middle of the thread and tie both ends in a double knot to secure them.

2 Position the button on top of the fabric in the place it originally was. Check that it lines up with the buttonhole on the other side of the coat.

3 Push the needle through the fabric from the inside of the garment, up into one of the holes of the button. Pull the thread tightly.

③

4 Position a toothpick on top of the button, between the holes.

5 Pass the thread over the toothpick and push the needle down through the hole opposite and then through the fabric.

6 Pass the needle up through the first hole again then back through the hole on the other side.

⑤

103

7 Continue sewing through each of the button's holes until you have done about fifteen stitches.

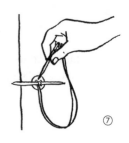

8 If your button has four holes, repeat **steps 6** and **7** on the other two holes. If your button is the kind with only two holes, continue to **step 9**.

9 Push the needle to the front of the fabric, so that your thread is now between the button and the fabric.

10 Carefully remove the toothpick and gently pull the button away from the garment—this will make a small space underneath. Wrap the thread around the space between the button and the fabric about twenty times.

11 Push the needle through to the back of the fabric.

12 Make several stitches in one place, then cut the thread.

Shank Buttons

Your button might have a small loop of metal or plastic on its back rather than four holes—this is called a shank.

If you're sewing on a button like this, you don't need to worry about **step 3** through **10**.

To start, push your needle through from the back of the garment; then thread it through the loop on the back of the button.

Make a small stitch in the fabric to secure the button in place. Then push the needle through the loop in the button, and make another stitch on top of the first one.

Repeat this four or five times, then finish with **steps 11** and **12**.

TEST A SMOKE ALARM

A smoke alarm is one of the most important things in your house. It could save your life! But a smoke alarm with a dead battery is totally useless. It's vital that you test it regularly to make sure it's working. Here's how.

● ●

1 Before you test the alarm, warn anyone in the house about what you're going to do so they don't think there's a real fire and call 911.

2 To reach the smoke alarm, use a chair or stepladder. Place it on a smooth, flat surface and ask a friend to hold it steady.

3 Look for the test button on your alarm. It's usually red. Press the button.

4 If the alarm and battery are both working, you should hear a loud beep or ring, and it might beep on and off for a while as it resets.

5 Note the date of your test and set a reminder for the next test date. If it isn't working, tell an adult in the house and ask them to replace the battery immediately.

⚠ WARNING

Never borrow the battery from a smoke alarm for use in anything else—you might forget to replace it!

THREAD A NEEDLE

Before you can make repairs to any of your clothes, you need to be able to thread a needle. Here's how to do it.

● ●

❶ Cut a piece of thread about the same length as your arm.

❷ Hold up the needle and tilt it so you can see the hole in it, called the eye. Take the freshly cut end of the thread and carefully push it through the eye—this might take a few tries.

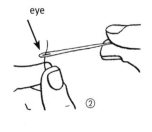

eye

②

❸ Once the thread comes out on the other side of the eye, take hold of it with the tips of your fingers and pull it until you have a "tail" of two to four inches.

tail

③

❹ Tie two knots on top of each other at the long end of the thread. This will stop the thread from being pulled all the way through the fabric while you're sewing. Now you're ready for any emergency sewing projects.

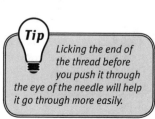

Tip

Licking the end of the thread before you push it through the eye of the needle will help it go through more easily.

TIE A BOWLINE

The bowline is used a lot on boats, but it's a helpful knot
to know in tons of situations. In fact, it's sometimes called
King of the Knots because it's so useful. Follow these steps
to master the King of the Knots!

● ●

1 Cross one end of the rope over the rest of the rope to make
a small loop.

①

2 Bring the end of the rope back through the loop from behind
and pull it through to create another, larger loop.

②

3 Cross the end that you've just pulled through behind the rest
of the rope.

③

4 Bring this end back to the front of the rope and push it through the first loop that you made.

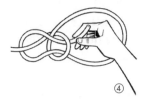

5 Pinch the end of the rope against the bottom of the larger loop and pull on the long end of the rope to tighten the knot.

Tip

It might seem childish, but if you find remembering how to tie a bowline is just too tricky, it might help you if you imagine the end of your rope is a mole. In order to tie a bowline, the mole needs to . . .

- *pop up out of his hole* (step 2)
- *run all the way around a tree* (steps 3 and 4)
- *pop back down into his hole* (steps 4 and 5)

TIE A CLOVE HITCH

A clove hitch is a useful knot to master for tying ropes around poles and railings. Here's how.

● ●

1 Wrap the rope twice over the railing, as shown.

2 Bring the left-hand end of the rope across to the right at the front of the railing.

3 Take the end of the rope in your left hand behind the railing and up.

4 Then tuck the end of the rope underneath the loop at the front and pull it tight, so it hangs down at the front of the railing, as shown here.

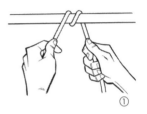

①

②

③

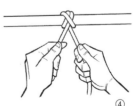

④

TIE A REEF KNOT

The reef knot is often used for tying bandages because it is so neat and flat. The ancient Greeks called it the Hercules Knot because it's so strong and useful. Be a mythical hero and learn how to tie one.

● ●

1 Take the two ends of a rope and cross end A over the top of end B, as shown.

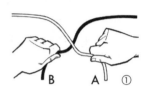

2 Tuck end A up behind end B. Then bring end B over the top of end A. Both ends should now be pointing upward, as shown here.

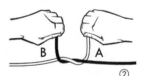

3 Bend end A back on itself, and bring end B over the top of it.

4 Tuck end B behind end A, and pull it through the loop that has formed.

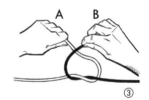

5 Pull both ends to tighten the knot.

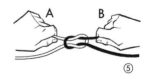

TIGHTEN A SCREW

Knowing how to use a screwdriver is a really useful skill for any number of projects. Here's how to tighten a screw.

● ●

1 Grip the handle of the screwdriver in your writing hand.

2 Place the end of the screwdriver into the notch on the screw head.

3 To tighten a screw, turn the screwdriver to the right (clockwise). To loosen a screw, turn the screwdriver to the left (counterclockwise). To remember which way you should turn the screwdriver to tighten a screw, use this rhyme: *Righty tighty, lefty loosey.*

4 Continue turning the screwdriver until the screw is held securely in place.

Before You Start

Check that your screwdriver is the right type and size for the screw you need to tighten. Here are the most common screw head shapes, and the screwdrivers that match them.

flat-head screwdriver

Phillips screwdriver

Part 6
Emergency Skills 101

Emergency situations can be pretty intense, but the key
is to remain calm instead of freaking out. If someone
is really in trouble and is not breathing or is bleeding
uncontrollably, call 911 ASAP. But if you or your friend
has a minor cut or splinter, you can totally help out!
Paging, Doctors McDreamy and McSteamy . . .

DEAL WITH MUSCLE CRAMPS

Have you ever woken up in the middle of the night
with your calf muscles feeling like they're on fire?
Cramps can come out of nowhere and can be very
painful when they strike. Read on to find out all
about cramps and how to stop them in their tracks.

● ●

WHAT IS A CRAMP?

A cramp is a muscle spasm. It can last just a few seconds or for
several minutes. It often occurs when muscles get tired, so is most
common during or after exercise. It does sometimes strike at
other times, too, such as when you are sleeping . . . Talk about a
rude awakening!

Leg Cramp

If the cramp is in your lower leg, take
your shoes off and flex your foot up
toward your shin, as shown here. This
will stretch the muscles in your leg and
stop them from cramping.

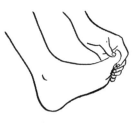

Arm Cramp

Lift the affected arm above your
head and bend it, reaching behind
you. Use the other hand to gently
push your arm down behind you by
pressing on your forearm just below
the elbow.

Post-Cramp Care

Figure out what is causing the cramp—for example, a pain in your hand from writing for a long time, or an arm ache from playing tennis. Once you've figured out the cause, take a break!

Massage the area where the cramp occurred by applying pressure with your hand and moving your hand over the area in small circles.

Prevent Cramps

Stretching your muscles before exercise can stop cramps before they strike. Here's how to stretch your legs.

1 Place the palms of your hands flat against a wall. Stand up and take a big step back with the right foot, then bend the left leg. Keep the right foot flat on the floor and straighten the leg until you can feel the stretch in your leg. Hold this position and count to ten.

①

2 Next, bring your right foot up until the heel of your shoe touches the back of your leg. Hold your ankle in this position and count to ten. Repeat **steps 1** and **2** with the other leg.

②

Tip

Cramps often occur due to dehydration, so drink plenty of water before and after exercising. Eating one banana a day can also help keep cramps at bay.

DRESS A CUT

Unless you wrap yourself in bubble wrap, cuts
and scrapes are going to happen. Here's how
to treat them so they heal quickly.

⚠ WARNING

*If the cut is deep or is longer than
half an inch, seek medical attention,
rather than trying to dress it yourself.
It may need stitches, which can only
be done by a medical professional.*

1 Wash and dry your hands thoroughly to minimize the risk of
infection (see Part 2 for hand-washing tips).

2 Put the cut area under lukewarm
running water to help clean the
injury. If you see gravel, splinters,
or pieces of glass caught in the
wound, ask someone for help.

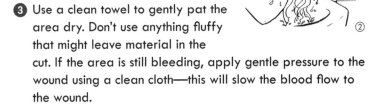

3 Use a clean towel to gently pat the
area dry. Don't use anything fluffy
that might leave material in the
cut. If the area is still bleeding, apply gentle pressure to the
wound using a clean cloth—this will slow the blood flow to
the wound.

4 If the cut or graze continues to bleed, raise the wounded area up. This should stop the bleeding.

5 Once the bleeding has stopped, apply a small blob of antiseptic cream to the area using a clean finger.

6 Choose a bandage with an absorbent pad that's large enough to cover the cut.

7 Put it over the cut and gently press the sticky areas down to fix it in place.

WARNING

If blood seeps through the bandage, apply another one over the top. If the bleeding continues, remove both dressings, apply fresh ones, and seek medical attention immediately.

Tip

If you don't have a bandage large enough to cover the wound, you can make your own by using a gauze bandage instead. Use bandage tape to fix the bandage in place.

EXTRACT A SPLINTER

Splinters are like paper cuts—tiny, minor annoyances that can actually be very painful! Here's how to get one out without making it hurt even more.

● ●

1 Wash your hands, and then gently wash the area around the splinter.

2 Stand under a light or by a window, and use a magnifying glass or a mirror to identify exactly where the splinter is. Once you have located it, use a clean pair of tweezers to gently pull

the splinter out. To do this, press the tweezers on your skin just under where the splinter is poking out. Hold the end of the splinter firmly in the tips of the tweezers and pull in the opposite direction that it went in. Don't press down directly on the splinter—this could push it deeper into your skin.

3 Once you have removed the splinter, wash and clean the whole area with mild antiseptic.

Tip

If the splinter isn't budging, take a hot bath or shower—the steam will open the skin's pores—then try again. If it still won't come out, you might need to have your doctor do it for you.

117

HELP A CHOKING VICTIM

**If a friend starts choking on a piece of food,
you need to act fast. Here's what to do.**

● ●

1 Tell him to cough—this may be enough to clear the blockage.

2 If your friend can't clear his throat by coughing, stand behind him. Explain that you are going to try to clear the blockage by sharply tapping him on the back five times.

3 Gently lean your friend forward and then give him five short, sharp whacks on the back with the heel of your hand. Check if the blockage has cleared after each whack. Repeat if necessary. If you have CPR training, you can also attempt the Heimlich maneuver.

4 If you still can't clear the blockage, tell your friend to stay calm while you dial 911.

⚠️

WARNING

If the person choking cannot speak or breathe, do not attempt to deal with it yourself. Call 911 immediately.

STOP A NOSEBLEED

If your nose is bleeding like you just got out of the ring with Rocky, follow these steps to stop it as soon as it starts.

● ●

1 Position an empty bucket on the floor just in front of a chair.

Tip
To avoid nosebleeds, only blow your nose when you need to and never blow too hard.

2 Sit down on the chair and lean forward slightly so that your nose is directly above the bucket. This way it will catch the dripping blood.

3 Firmly pinch the softest part of your nose—just above the nostrils and below the bony ridge—with your thumb and index finger. Breathe through your mouth.

4 Stay in this position for ten to fifteen minutes. The bleeding should stop during this period.

5 Avoid blowing your nose or bending down for a few hours after the bleeding stops.

WARNING

Go see a doctor if . . .

• *your nosebleed was caused by a fall or injury.*
• *you get nosebleeds very often.*
• *your nose continues to bleed heavily for more than thirty minutes.*

TAKE A PULSE

Taking a pulse will tell you more than just if a person's heart is beating or not. If they're hurt, the speed of someone's pulse can tell you more about their injuries. Here's how to take your own pulse.

● ●

1 Hold out one hand, with your palm facing up and your arm relaxed.

2 Put your index and middle finger on the inside of your wrist, near the thumb and just below the crease where the hand meets the arm. You will feel your pulse in beats. These beats are actually the blood moving underneath your skin.

> **Tip**
>
> *If you can't find a pulse at the wrist, put your index and middle fingers on the side of your neck below the jawline.*

3 When you've found your pulse, keep constant pressure on the spot with your fingers, and count the number of beats you feel in ten seconds. Multiply the number you get by six to work out how many beats your pulse makes in a minute.

> **?**
>
> ### Did you know...
>
> *A resting heart rate (your heart rate when you have just woken up in the morning) can be anywhere between sixty and a hundred beats per minute. If your pulse rate worries you, tell an adult or your doctor.*

③

TREAT A BEE STING

Ah, summer—baseball, the beach, and . . . bees! A bee sting
can be painful, but here's how to treat it.

● ●

1 First you need to remove the
stinger that the bee has left
behind inside your skin. Bee stings
have tiny hooks called barbs on
them that can get stuck in your skin
if you just pull them out. To avoid
this, scrape the edge of a ruler or
a credit card in a scooping motion across the sting to
gradually ease it out.

2 Wash the area with soap and water, and dry it gently. The
area around the sting may be swollen and throbbing—don't
worry, this is normal.

3 Wrap some ice cubes or an ice
pack in a towel and place it on
the stung area.

4 Rest the area that has been
stung and elevate it if you can
to reduce any swelling.

> ⚠️
> **WARNING**
>
> *If your eyes, lips, or tongue swell, or
> you feel dizzy or it's hard to breathe,
> you may be allergic to the sting. Get
> help from an adult immediately.*

TREAT A BURN

If you burn or scald your skin, you need to act fast to stop more damage from occurring. Here's how.

● ●

1 Get away from the cause of the burn.

2 Run some cool, but not freezing, tap water. Be careful not to have the tap turned on fully—the pressure of the water might damage the skin further.

WARNING

If the burn is bigger than three inches, or if the skin is broken, do not attempt to treat it yourself. Seek medical attention immediately.

3 Place the burned area under the cool water. If the burned area is on your leg, use the bath tap or shower instead of the sink.

WARNING

Never use carbonated drinks, ice cubes, or ointments on the burned area.

4 Hold the burned area under the running water for ten to fifteen minutes.

5 Loosely rest a gauze bandage or a dampened dressing over the burn. If you don't have gauze, use a clean plastic bag for an injured hand or use a clean piece of plastic wrap for scalded arms and legs. Don't wrap it too tightly, in case the burn swells up.

Authors

Martin Oliver
Since starting his career as an author, Martin Oliver has written over twenty books for children that cover subjects as wide-ranging as pirates, pharaohs, and puzzle adventures. He's also written two titles in the Popular Knowledge series, *Dead Dinosaurs* and *Groovy Movies*. Martin lives in Teddington, near London, with his wife, Andrea, and their two daughters, Katie and Isabelle.

Alexandra Johnson
Alexandra Johnson is the pseudonym for Gemma Reece, author of the bestselling *Girls' Book of Friendship* and *Girls' Book of Secrets*. She lives in the UK.

97 Things to Do Before You Finish High School

by Steven Jenkins and Erika Stalder

$9.99 • ISBN: 978-0-9790173-0-8
Paperback, 208 pages, 2c, 6½ x 6½, Ages 14+

NAPPA Honors Award

Don't Sit On the Baby

The Ultimate Guide to Sane, Skilled, and Safe Babysitting

by Halley Bondy

$12.99 • ISBN: 978-0-9827322-3-6
Paperback, 128 pages, 2c, 5½ x 7½, Ages 12+

Holy Spokes!

A Biking Bible for Everyone

by Rob Coppolillo

$14.99 • ISBN: 978-1-936976-23-2
Paperback, 208 pages, 2c, 5½ x 7½, Ages 12+

47 Things You Can Do for the Environment

by Lexi Petronis with environmental consultant Jill Buck, founder of Go Green Initiative

$10.99 • ISBN: 978-0-9827322-1-2
Paperback, 128 pages, 2c, 6½ x 6½, Ages 12+

Start It Up

The Complete Teen Business Guide to Turning Your Passions Into Pay

by Kenrya Rankin

$14.99 • ISBN: 978-0-9819733-5-7
Paperback, 160 pages, 2c, 7 x 8, Ages 12+

Where's My Stuff?

The Ultimate Teen Organizing Guide

by Samantha Moss, with teen organizer Lesley Schwartz

$12.99 • ISBN: 978-0-9819733-7-1
Paperback, 104 pages, 4c, 6½ x 8½, Ages 12+